W9-CCC-632

Fall
Colors

Brian Enslow

Enslow Elementary

an imprint of

Enslow Publishers, Inc.
40 Industrial Road
Box 398
Berkeley Heights, NJ 07922
USA

http://www.enslow.com

Alexander Mitchell Library
Aberdeen, SD 57401
DISCARDED
3219459

Enslow Elementary, an imprint of Enslow Publishers, Inc.

Enslow Elementary® is a registered trademark of Enslow Publishers, Inc.

Copyright © 2012 by Enslow Publishers, Inc.

All rights reserved.

No part of this book may be reproduced by any means
without the written permission of the publisher.

Library of Congress Cataloging-in-Publication Data

Enslow, Brian.
  Fall colors / Brian Enslow.
    p. cm.
  Includes index.
  Summary: "Learn about colors while looking at pictures of fall"— Provided by publisher.
  ISBN 978-0-7660-3909-4
  1. Autumn—Juvenile literature. 2. Color—Juvenile literature. I. Title.
  QB637.7.E57 2012
  508.2—dc23   2011014447

Paperback ISBN: 978-1-59845-264-8

Printed in the United States of America

052011 Lake Book Manufacturing, Inc., Melrose Park, IL

10 9 8 7 6 5 4 3 2 1

To Our Readers: We have done our best to make sure all Internet Addresses in this book were active and appropriate when we went to press. However, the author and the publisher have no control over and assume no liability for the material available on those Internet sites or on other Web sites they may link to.

✪ Enslow Publishers, Inc., is committed to printing our books on recycled paper. The paper in every book contains 10% to 30% post-consumer waste (PCW). The cover board on the outside of each book contains 100% PCW. Our goal is to do our part to help young people and the environment too!

Photo Credits: Antonio-1/Shutterstock.com, p. 8; burly/Shutterstock.com, p. 10; fdenb/Shutterstock.com, p. 18; mahout/Shutterstock.com, p. 12; Martin Fowler/Shutterstock.com, p. 14; mirounga/Shutterstock.com, p. 23; Monkey Business Images/Shutterstock.com, p. 1; Perrush/Shutterstock.com, p. 16; Quicksnap Photo/Shutterstock.com, p. 20; Stephen Rudolph/Shutterstock.com, p. 4; Tony Campbell/Shutterstock.com, p. 21; Yellowj/Shutterstock.com, p. 7.

Cover Photo: Monkey Business Images/Shutterstock.com

Note to Parents and Teachers

Help pre-readers get a jumpstart on reading. These **simple texts** introduce **new concepts** with repetition of words and **short simple phrases**. Photos and illustrations fill the pages with color and effectively enhance the text. Free Educator Guides are available for this series at www.enslow.com. Search for the **All About Colors of the Seasons** series by name.

Contents

Words to Know

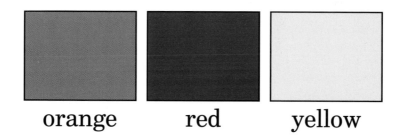

orange   red   yellow

brown

red

green

orange

yellow

purple

blue

5

red apple

orange
pumpkin

yellow leaf

green
acorns

blue berries

15

purple hat

brown boat

white dog

black cat

What colors do you see?

Happy Halloween!

Read More

Eckart, Edana. *Watching the Seasons*. New York, NY: Children's Press. 2004.

Mueller, Gerda. *Autumn*. Edinburgh, UK: Floris Books. 2004.

Web Sites

KidsGeo
<http://www.kidsgeo.com/geography-for-kids/0017-the-earths-movements.php>

KidZone
<http://www.kidzone.ws/science/colorwheel.htm>

Index

Guided Reading Level: **B**
Guided Reading Leveling System is based on the guidelines recommended by Fountas and Pinnell.

Word Count: **28**